MERSEYSIDE TRACTION

Doug Birmingham

AMBERLEY

Front cover: In Tata silver livery, No. 60099 approaches Ropers Bridge, Whiston, with a diverted 6F78, the 11.30 Fiddlers Ferry Power Station to Liverpool Bulk Terminal empty HTA hoppers. In the background is the author's local station, Whiston, which was built and opened in 1990. 16 April 2012.

Rear cover: In attractive Rail Operations Group livery, Class 37 No. 37884 passes Halewood on the Up slow line with 5V94, the 10.00 Allerton Depot to Long Marston ECS (Empty Coaching Stock), on 25 October 2017. The stock consists of ex-Thameslink Class 319 EMU No. 319421, which was going to Long Marston for storage pending further operation on the network.

First published 2018

Amberley Publishing
The Hill, Stroud
Gloucestershire, GL5 4EP

www.amberley-books.com

Copyright © Doug Birmingham, 2018

The right of Doug Birmingham to be identified as the Author of this work has been asserted in accordance with the Copyrights, Designs and Patents Act 1988.

ISBN 978 1 4456 7554 1 (print)
ISBN 978 1 4456 7555 8 (ebook)

British Library Cataloguing in Publication Data. A catalogue record for this book is available from the British Library.

Origination by Amberley Publishing.
Printed in the UK.

Introduction

Mention Liverpool and Merseyside conjures up many thoughts and images of the people and the area, certainly the Beatles, football, the Docks, the River Mersey, the Ferries and of course the people too, with their distinctive dialect and humour. However, probably with the exception of the Third Rail self-contained railway system, railway enthusiasts, let alone the general public, may not think the area would be deeply associated with railways! Nevertheless, the area is steeped in railway history with the famous Rainhill locomotive trials in 1829 and the birth of what we know as intercity passenger travel a year later with the Liverpool & Manchester Railway created by George Stephenson linking both these cities together. Beyond that, you have the famous Vulcan Foundry at Newton-le-Willows, which produced steam, diesel and electric locomotives, not just for the UK but all across the world too. Other examples of railway history include the Mersey Railway, the forerunner to the Merseyrail system, the Liverpool Overhead Railway (affectionately known as the Dockers' Umbrella), Edge Hill's famous Gridiron, and the boat trains to and from Liverpool Riverside Station among many other historic subjects and locations. With the above in mind, one could be forgiven for creating an illustrated history to show that in this publication, but there are many authors who have covered the railway history of Liverpool and Merseyside in the past and whose knowledge and facts would far exceed those of the author. In the circumstances, it was decided to concentrate on the recent past and present day activities within the area of Merseyside.

When the author was approach by the publishers to compile his first book, they kindly let the author decide the time span to cover, along with the contents to be chosen. At the outset, a decision was made to cover the last twenty years, as anything shorter or longer probably would not be able to do any kind of justice to the area as a whole. As the book title suggests, the emphasis would normally be on using the county boundaries as the start and finishing point but it is a little misleading as the local passenger transport executive, Merseytravel, actually goes beyond the county boundaries and also now covers the Borough of Halton as part of the newly created Liverpool City Region. So, for clarity, the author has used the Merseytravel boundaries, but not including the Borough of Halton, as the extent of choosing the contents of this book. The locations do include Southport, Ormskirk, Rainford, St Helens, Newton-le-Willows, Hough Green (Widnes) and Halewood, all of which are north of the River Mersey, and those on the other side of the river include New Brighton, West Kirby, Upton, Hooton and Ellesmere Port.

As mentioned before, Merseyside tends to be ignored by railway enthusiasts as it is automatically associated with the widespread Merseyrail system currently operated by Class 507 and 508 EMUs, and with some justification. However, like many areas of the country, Merseyside has its fair share of numerous passenger and freight trains and surprisingly there is much variety when it comes to the diesel and electric traction that has appeared on a regular basis, as well as the odd welcomed visitor too. Certainly when compiling this book, at least twenty-six locomotive classes have been recorded as well as the appearance of twenty-two classes of multiple units, most of which are regular visitors to the area. Merseyside is currently regularly served by seven Train Operating Companies, including Arriva Wales, Arriva North, East Midlands Trains, London Midland, Merseyrail, Trans-Pennine Express and Virgin Trains, with three Freight Operating Companies operating daily in and out of the area including DB Cargo, Freightliner and GBRf. However, Colas, Direct Rail Services, Network Rail, Rail Operations Group and West Coast Railways do pass through the area too. So there is much variety to be recorded and that does not include the amount of liveries that have appeared too.

As for the railway lines covered, we will begin with Merseyrail. This is a self-contained third rail 750 DC commuter system split into two zones, with Liverpool City Centre being the hub of the lines; one zone is the Wirral line, which serves New Brighton, West Kirby, Chester and Ellesmere Port and the other zone is the Northern line, serving Hunts Cross, Southport, Ormskirk and Kirkby. Although there is no traction variety on the system, the infrastructure at many of the stations dates back to the pre-BR days and it is consequently worth recording. There are three main lines serving Liverpool city centre, which include the former Liverpool & Manchester Railway via Rainhill to Manchester Victoria, along with the line to St Helens Central and beyond. There are also the former London & North Western Railway to Runcorn, Crewe and London and the Cheshire Lines Committee line to Warrington Central and Manchester Piccadilly. Other active lines in Merseyside include the Bootle Branch Line, which serves Liverpool Docks, as well as a small portion of the West Coast Main Line as it passes through Newton-le-Willows. Sadly, three other lines within the county, although (just) still present, no longer see any traffic and are now succumbing to nature – the line to Birkenhead Docks, the North Mersey Branch (Bootle Junction to Aintree), and the Ravenhead Branch (St Helens Station Junction to Sutton). There are a handful of images in this publication taken on the latter two lines.

There are a number of locations where freight trains originate and are covered in this publication, which include Liverpool Docks, where traffic currently includes biomass, scrap and steel. In the past coal and intermodal trains also served the Docks, but the latter are set to return sometime in 2018. There are three locations served in the south of Liverpool, these being the Garston Freightliner terminal, Garston Auto Terminal and Halewood, serving the Jaguar/Land Rover factory. Other locations served are Knowsley Freight Terminal in Kirkby (domestic waste) and Ravenhead, St Helens (sand). Sadly, there is no freight serving the Wirral, although Ellesmere Port had coal, biomass and sand trains until 2016, which are covered in this book.

With the exception of two images, all images in this book have all been taken by the author and cover a period from 1998 to 2017, as well as two images taken in 1995 and 1996 for added interest. They have been chosen to represent a wide variety of locations, liveries and traction, not just locomotives but also a small selection of multiple units too, as they are a major part of the current railway scene. It is inevitable that some readers may suggest one or two subjects may be missing in this publication but hopefully a broad overview has been achieved, including some past and present views representing some of the infrastructure changes in Merseyside.

I would like to dedicate some images in this publication to Stuart Daniels, who sadly passed away in May 2016 aged forty-four years. He was a good friend of over twenty-four years, a popular and respected employee at EWS and latterly GBRf. Nothing was ever too much trouble for Stuart, who was always helping his friends and colleagues, and without his assistance on many an occasion the author would have not known of some freight workings and obtaining the images would have been impossible too. Thank you Stu – you will be sadly missed by all.

Further images are available to view via the author's website, www.8arail.uk, by clicking on the appropriate Flickr links.

Doug Birmingham, Liverpool
December 2017

As an introduction to this book, this is one of my favourite steam images of all time, when circumstances came together with the sun appearing just at the right time! It is nice when this happens, which makes the time and effort in our hobby worthwhile. LMS-built Coronation Class locomotive No. 46233 *Duchess of Sutherland*, resplendent in BR Brunswick green, approaches Huyton station with 1Z30, the 16.11 Carlisle via Liverpool Lime Street to Crewe 'Cumbrian Mountain Express' Railtour. *Duchess of Sutherland,* a few minutes later, would be passing the site of her former home in the early 1960s, Edge Hill (8A) steam shed. 28 July 2012.

History was made on 19 July 1998 when for the first and only occasion Class 201 DEMU Hastings unit No. 1001 visited Liverpool Lime Street station. This occurred as the Hastings unit had been chartered to transport VSOE passengers from Edge Hill station to Hillside station on the Merseyrail Northern line in connection with the Royal Birkdale Open Golf Tournament on 17 and 18 July. No. 1001 is seen at Platform 6 prior to departure to Norwich.

West Coast Railways Class 37 No. 37668 passes Liverpool Lime Street Signal Box with 5Z95, the 08.30 Crewe DRS to Liverpool Lime St empty coach stock working in connection with the Railway Touring Company's excursion to Carlisle headed by ex-BR Jubilee Class steam locomotive No. 45690 *Leander*. The signal box will become redundant when signalling for the station is transferred to Manchester Rail Operating Centre in 2019. 24 July 2016.

Rebuilt by Brush Traction in 2012, No. 57305 *Northern Princess*, resplendent in Northern Belle livery, passes through Edge Hill station on 15 March 2015 with 1Z33, the 11.00 Chester to Shrewsbury Dining special. Edge Hill station is one of the world's oldest passenger stations and the buildings date back to 1836, when the station was first opened.

Taken during an official visit to Alstom Edge Hill Depot, this excellent facility completes the daily maintenance of the Pendolino fleet and is able to accommodate two eleven-car Class 390 units. In view is No. 390010 *The Cumbrian Spirit*, which became the first Pendolino to receive the new interim 'white' livery in September 2017. Alongside is No. 390135 *City of Lancaster*, which was receiving replacement doors as well as routine maintenance. 15 September 2015. (Image reproduced with kind permission of Alstom and Virgin Trains)

Freightliner Class 66 No. 66569 passes through Mossley Hill station on the up slow line with a diverted 4F80 Felixstowe to Garston FLT 'liner'. This train had been diverted via Earlestown, Rainhill and Edge Hill Wapping due to ongoing engineering work on the line between Weaver Junction and Speke Junction. 20 September 2008.

Built by General Motors Alstom at Valencia, Spain, in 2000, EWS livery Class 67 No. 67003 heads 5T89, the 17.15 Crewe Carriage Sidings to Liverpool Lime Street 'VSOE' ECS. The VSOE stock was on its annual visit to the area which brings passengers from London Victoria in connection with the Grand National horse race at Aintree Racecourse. Classmate No. 67008 provided the motive power for the return to London Victoria station. 9 April 2011.

On loan to Virgin Trains, two-tone grey Freightliner livery No. 90142 powers 1F17, the 12.50 London Euston to Liverpool Lime Street station train, on the Down fast line through Mossley Hill station. Class 90 No. 90142 was built at Crewe Works in 1990 as No. 90042 but was renumbered to 90142 in July 1991 as part of the dedicated fleet of freight locomotives for Freightliner. It subsequently reverted back to No. 90042 in 2001, now in Freightliner Powerhaul livery. 31 July 1999.

On Sunday 14 May 2017, a rare visit was made to the area by two London Midland Class 170 units, Nos 170501 and 170505, which were chartered by the Cotswold Line Rail User Group for a day visit to Liverpool and marketed under the title of 'Wye Mersey Express'. The two units are seen passing through Mossley Hill station with 5T71, the 16.52 Crewe to Liverpool Lime St ECS. They had been stabled at Crewe for servicing between the inward and outward journeys.

Just like old times (well, almost) as LMS Princess Class locomotive No. 6201 *Princess Elizabeth* heads Past Time Rail's 'Merseyside Express' railtour from London Euston to Liverpool Lime Street, passing through West Allerton station on the final leg of its journey. This was a proud moment for the photographer as the fireman looking out of the cab was his son, Christopher, who had fired *Lizzie* from Bescot. Saturday 10 February 2007.

In EWS Railway Executive silver livery, No. 67029 *Royal Diamond* passes through West Allerton station with the EWS Management train after a visit to Liverpool Lime Street station on 8 July 2011. The locomotive was named in 2007 in honour of the 60th wedding anniversary of Queen Elizabeth ll and Prince Phillip. At the time of writing she is part of the Arriva Wales West pool of locomotives.

Diesel-hydraulic Type 4 D1015 *Western Champion* heads 1Z52, the 17.43 Liverpool Lime Street to Salisbury 'The Festival of the Sea' Pathfinder railtour, through West Allerton station on 21 July 2008. D1015 is currently the only certified mainline Western and had brought passengers to the area in connection with the visit of the Tall Ships during the successful Liverpool European Capital of Culture year celebrations.

Previously named *Abertawe/Landore* and *Great Western*, Class 47 No. 47815, operated by Rail Operations Group, hauls 5V67, the 12.17 Allerton Depot to Long Marston ECS, on the slow line through West Allerton station. The stock comprised two former Thameslink Class 319 EMUs, Nos 319218 and 219, which had been at Allerton for storage. However, both units, operated by Rail Operations Group, unusually did make one return journey to and from Liverpool Lime Street station under their own power before they were transferred to Long Marston. 15 March 2017.

Network Rail's New Measurement Train, consisting of two Class 43 power cars powered by Paxman Valenta engines at that time (Nos 43062 and 43014), and six Mk 3 coaches, is seen here as it approaches West Allerton station with 1Z92, the 11.19 Glasgow Central to Liverpool Lime St station 'Test' train. Network Rail has three Class 43 power cars in total, with No. 43013 being the third one, now powered by MTU engines, with the train operating up and down the country to check the condition of the running lines. 3 May 2008.

Approaching Liverpool South Parkway station on 18 March 2008, Network Rail's Class 31 No. 31105 heads south with 5Z47, the Liverpool Lime Street to Derby Railway Technical Centre ECS, including DBSO No. 9703. The locomotive was built in 1959 by Brush Traction as D5523 and was renumbered to 31105 at the end of 1973, until withdrawal in 1997. However, it was reinstated in 2002 and became part of the Network Rail locomotive fleet.

Freightliner Class 66 No. 66504 passes through Allerton station with 4K53, the 11.26 Seaforth Container Terminal to Crewe Basford Hall liner, on 4 March 2000. Since this image was taken Allerton station (along with nearby Garston station) has been transformed into a major interchange station and renamed Liverpool South Parkway station, serving numerous TOCs along with nearby Liverpool John Lennon Airport.

Former Virgin Thunderbird Class 57 No. 57312 *Peter Henderson* with No. 57306 leading five Autoballasters through Liverpool South Parkway station with 6G30, the 16.30 Bootle Branch Junction to Crewe Basford Hall hoppers. Nowadays No. 57312 is operated by DRS in Northern Belle livery and is named *Solway Princess*. 27 April 2014.

Once a year on Grand National day, East Midlands Trains normally substitute two Class 158 DMUs with a Class 222 Meridian seven-car DMU due to the increased number of passengers visiting Aintree Racecourse. On 14 April 2012, No. 222003 is seen arriving at Liverpool South Parkway station with 1Z90, the 15.45 Nottingham to Liverpool Lime Street train.

Ex-Southern EMU No. 508103, in the Merseyrail silver livery, with a Southport to Hunts Cross train prepares to stop at Platform 5 of the new Liverpool South Parkway station, which replaced both Allerton and Garston stations. The latter ex-CLC station is seen in the background beyond the bridge, a few months before it was demolished. 17 July 2006.

On the former Cheshire Lines Committee line from Liverpool Central to Manchester Central station, and in new Merseyrail livery, No. 508136 arrives at Aigburth station with 2U29, the 12.43 Southport to Hunts Cross train, on 7 August 2015. Above the train is the original station master's house and booking office, with the canopy still in place on the Southport-bound platform.

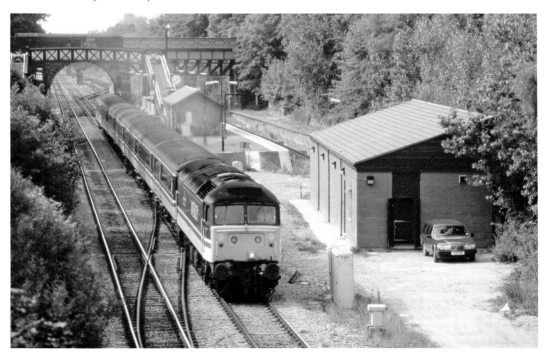

Taken from Mackets Lane Bridge, Class 47 No. 47845 *County of Kent* passes the red brick building of Hunts Cross Signal Box on the 13.26 Liverpool Lime St to London Paddington Cross Country diversion. No. 47845 was rebuilt as a Class 57, initially numbered 57611 before becoming No. 57301, and nowadays is named *Goliath* in DRS two-tone blue livery. 10 September 1995.

Although Hough Green station, Widnes, is in the County of Cheshire, the station comes under the 'Merseytravel' transport area as noted by the station sign. Virgin Trains Thunderbird No. 57303 *Alan Tracy* in original form is seen here passing the former CLC station with the 12.09 Liverpool Lime Street to London Euston diversion on 22 April 2004. No. 57303, currently in DRS livery named *Pride of Carlisle*, was also No. 47705 as part of the ScotRail push/pull fleet, named *Lothian* at the time, as well as being in LNWR black livery while named *Guy Fawkes*.

This Merseytravel station does not see many loco-hauled trains on the former CLC route except for the very occasional diversion, but on one such other occasion, DRS Class 37 No. 37667 is seen passing Hough Green station with 1Q14, the 08.52 Derby Railway Technical Centre to Crewe Network Rail test train, with fellow classmate No. 37194 on the rear. 17 September 2012.

Probably the first image taken of newly painted Class 33 No. 33030 in EWS livery, which was completed during the previous week at Allerton T&RS Depot. The locomotive arrived at the depot in Civil Engineers livery and departed to Crewe the day after this image was taken, hauled by No. 90134, before carrying on to Toton Depot for the Open Weekend. '8J' on the head-code blind refers to Allerton's Shed code in late BR steam days. 26 August 1998.

Large loco livery Class 37 No. 37425 *Pride of the Valleys/Balchder y Cymoedd* inside Allerton T&RS Depot being used as the depot shunter, while in the background are two withdrawn Class 08s, No. 08397 and 08954, awaiting their fate. Happily, No. 37425 is now operated by DRS and reverted to its previous name of *Sir Robert McAlpine/Concrete Bob*. 22 March 2008.

EWS Class 67 No. 67002 shunts ex-6X41, the 00.32 Dagenham RS auto train, at Garston Car Terminal while No. 66124 stables on the shunt line. This train had been unusually diverted via Earlestown, Rainhill and Edge Hill Wapping due to engineering work on the ex-LNWR line via Runcorn, with both locomotives top and tailing the train. 20 September 2008.

On 22 June 2016, the Queen and the Duke of Edinburgh visited Liverpool in connection with the opening of the new Alder Hey Children's Hospital and also the New Exhibition Centre. They had travelled by the Royal Train to Lime St station having been stabled at Hooton station the previous evening. Passing Halewood West Junction are DBC revised livery Royal Class 67s No. 67005 *Queens Messenger* with No. 67006 *Royal Sovereign* at the rear on an ECS to Wolverton Works.

In Powerhaul Freightliner livery, No. 70013, built by General Electric (USA) in 2011, passes Halewood West Junction with Saturdays-only 4K45, the 12.52 Ditton to Crewe Basford Hall liner, which travels via Speke Junction for operational purposes. This location is now sadly inaccessible as a fenced car park was built for Jaguar/Land Rover employees. 6 August 2016.

Looking good in her new Freightliner Powerhaul livery, Class 90, No. 90042 passes Halewood East Junction with 4K64, the 11.46 Garston Freightliner Terminal to Crewe Basford Hall liner. This particular daily Freightliner train always produces a variety of motive power including Class 66, Class 70 and Class 86, single or double-headed, as well as the Class 90s. 23 February 2015.

Virgin Trains Class 47 No. 47827 creates a spray as it approaches Halewood East Junction on the 06.40 Poole to Liverpool Lime Street station cross-country service in rare snowy winter conditions. The Class 47 was eventually rebuilt by Brush Traction as No. 57302 in July 2002 and named *Virgil Tracy* as part of the Virgin Trains Thunderbird fleet. Later on it became part of DRS and was renamed *Chad Varah*. 29 December 2009.

In 'Alphaline' livery, an Express Sprinter Class 158, No. 158835, approaches Halewood East Junction with a Cardiff Central to Liverpool Lime Street express service. 'Alphaline' came about in 1990 as a brand to advertise Regional Railways 'express' services in the Midlands, Wales and the south-west of the country but eventually faded out. 22 December 2001.

In ex Thameslink livery, Class 319 EMU No. 319380 passes Halewood East Junction with 5Z20, the Allerton Depot to Crewe station driver training ECS. The Class 319 EMU had been transferred to the area along with a number of its classmates in preparation for the full electrification of the Liverpool and Manchester route operated by Northern Rail, and repainted in their attractive 'Northern Electric' livery. 4 January 2015.

Rekindling what was once a daily scene, in Caledonian Sleeper blue livery Class 87 No. 87002 *Royal Sovereign* approaches Halewood East Junction with 1Z82, the 14.20 London Euston to Liverpool Lime Street 'Footex' bringing Chelsea supporters for the game against Liverpool FC. No. 87002 normally operates the Caledonian Sleeper coach stock in and out of London Euston but occasionally it is allowed to stretch its legs on the WCML. 11 May 2016.

Built by General Motors, La Grange, Illinois, USA, in 1994, Class 59 No. 59201 was the first built of six Class 59/2s for National Power, before being transferred to EWS in 1998. EWS operated the Class 59/2s on a variety of workings including a period in Merseyside. Seen here is No59201 *Vale of York* approaching Halewood East Junction on 6F78, the 11.30 Fiddlers Ferry power station to Liverpool Bulk Terminal empty coal, on 10 February 2010.

In unique Powder Blue livery and named *Teenage Spirit*, Class 60 No. 60074 approaches Halewood East Junction on 6F78, the 11.30 Fiddlers Ferry power station to Liverpool Bulk Terminal empty HTAs. In the background are the cooling towers of the power station, where the train travels to Latchford Sidings, Arpley, before retracing its journey and passing the power station, finally heading for Liverpool. 4 January 2013

Not all is what it seems to be at Halewood as No. 66413 in Direct Rail Services livery powers Freightliner Saturdays only 4K45, the 12.52 Ditton to Crewe Basford Hall liner, which travels via Speke Junction for run round purposes. The Class 66 had been leased to Freightliner along with six other Class 66s by Direct Rail Services and now incorporated as part of their Intermodal fleet. 24 March 2012.

A new service that commenced in 2017 to Merseyside was stone from Peak Forest when Tarmac Construction opened a new stone terminal at Garston Freightliner Terminal. Freightliner won the contract to transport the stone and on its second day of operation, No. 66549 approaches Halewood East Junction on 6F70, the 09.56 Tunstead Sidings to Garston Tarmac Terminal. 11 May 2017.

Virgin Pendolino No. 390117 *Virgin Prince* on the down fast line approaches Halewood at speed on the last leg of its journey from London Euston to Liverpool Lime Street. At that time Alstom and Virgin Trains were sponsors of the London 2012 Olympics and some of the Pendolinos had the names of various British athletes on the nose of the units. In this instance, the name of long jumper Abigail Irozuru was on No. 390117, as seen in this image. 17 November 2012.

With the backdrop of the A561 road bridge crossing the railway, London Midland Class 350 EMU No. 350256 on the Up fast line overtakes EWS livery Class 66 No. 66091. The latter had just departed from Halewood Exchange Sidings with 6O42, the 11.31 to Southampton East Docks Land Rover auto train. The Class 350 was on 1L76, the 12.04 Liverpool Lime Street to Birmingham New Street, with the train's next stop being only five minutes away, at Runcorn station. 11 May 2017

On a nice winter's day, and framed in a neighbour's driveway, Freightliner's Class 86s Nos 86639 and 86638, and Class 66 No. 66956 travel light engine from Garston Freightliner Terminal to Ditton Reception Sidings, where the two Class 86s will take forward 4L92, the 14.02 liner to Felixstowe. This location, Higher Road, Halebank, is in Cheshire, although the railway runs through Knowsley, Merseyside. 18 February 2016.

Late spring in each year always produces plenty of colour with rapeseed fields being prominent and always providing an image when they are next to railway lines around the UK. Within a few metres of the previous image on Higher Road, EWS livery Class 66 No. 66135 passes with 6O42, the 11.31 Halewood to Southampton Eastern Docks Land Rover auto train. 13 May 2015.

As part of the GBRf Class 92 UK Sleeper and Channel Tunnel fleet, No. 92044 *Couperin* passes the site of the old Halebank station with 6X43, the 09.45 Dagenham Dock Reception Sidings to Garston Car Terminal auto train comprising new Ford vehicles, on 2 February 2016. This train operates as required and, depending on the time of year, runs once a week, arriving late afternoon at the terminal.

New to the shores of the UK in the last few years, built by Vossloh España, Albuixech (Valencia), Spain, for Direct Rail Services, are Class 68 No. 68004 *Rapid* with No. 68002 *Intrepid* on the rear of 1Q18, the 09.30 Crewe via Liverpool Lime St to Crewe Network Rail test train, as it approaches the site of the old Halebank station. This particular train tends to make two round trips to Liverpool in order to inspect both the fast and slow lines in the area. 18 February 2016.

In late afternoon winter sunlight, Freightliner No. 66567 travels the Down fast line on 4O29, the 15.12 Garston Freightliner Terminal to Southampton Maritime Container Terminal liner, as it approaches the site of the old Halebank station. This station comprised four platforms, opened by the St Helens Railway in 1852 and closed by British Railways in 1958, with only the station house still in existence. 2 December 2014.

Built by Brush Traction, Loughborough, in 1996 as part of a fleet of forty-six for mainly Channel Tunnel traffic, Class 92 No. 92043 *Debussey,* now in GBRf blue livery, approaches Halebank with 6L48, the 15.49 Garston Car Terminal to Dagenham Dock Reception Sidings empty auto train. This service was previously operated by DBS until 21 February 2014, when GBRf took over the contract. 8 October 2015.

DBC Class 60 No. 60066 in Drax Powering Tomorrow silver livery starts the first leg of its journey to Southampton Eastern Docks as it approaches Lower Road, Halebank, with 6O42, the 11.31 from Halewood. With the exception of a handful of occasions this train, loaded with Land Rover Evoques and Discoveries worth over £3 million in total, is normally hauled by a Class 66. 28 January 2014.

Who would have thought in 2017 that Class 86s would still be reliably hauling trains on a daily basis after over fifty years in service? Here we have two Freightliner Class 86s, Nos 86605 and 86638, built in 1965, on a very colourful 4K64, the 11.46 Garston FLT to Crewe Basford Hall liner, passing Manor Farm Fields, Halebank, on 17 March 2016. It is not uncommon to see Class 66s, Class 70s and Class 90s, as well as single Class 86s, on this particular Freightliner service.

Although this image is actually taken in Ellesmere Port, Cheshire, this location is on the boundary of the Merseytravel area and is served by Merseyrail Class 507 and 508 EMUs. Passing the station building, which was under renovation, GBRf Class 66 No. 66739 *Bluebell Railway* approaches the link to Ellesmere Port docks, the destination for 4F70, the ex-13.00 Ironbridge power station empty biomass, on 26 June 2013.

Freightliner heavyhaul Class 66 No. 66616 powers away past Ellesmere Port station with 6F02, the 12.15 Manistry Wharf to Fiddlers Ferry power station coal. This train initially started out being hauled by Class 66s, and was then eventually taken over on a daily basis by Class 70s. Eventually the service ceased with the closure of Manistry Wharf to all rail traffic, along with the demand for coal for power stations. 26 September 2007.

In original silver Merseyrail livery, Class 507 EMU No. 507024 is awaiting to depart Ellesmere Port station for Liverpool Central station, as Northern Rail Class 156 DMU No. 156486 has departed with the limited daily service to and from Helsby station. At that time the DMU would have gone ECS to and from Liverpool Lime Street or Chester stations to Helsby station. 7 September 2012.

Class 508 EMU No. 508125 is awaiting to depart Hooton station with a train to Chester station from Liverpool Central. The unit is in original Merseyrail black/grey stripe livery, and since this image was taken the station has had a major renovation, which included a new footbridge with lifts to comply with disabled access legislation. 29 March 2002.

On 6 July 2013, Northern Rail and the North Cheshire Rail Users Group joined together to celebrate the 150th anniversary of the Hooton to Helsby line, which opened on 1 July 1863, and for the occasion two Class 156 units, Nos 156423 and 156425, were used on the Liverpool Lime Street to Hooton and return railtour. Seen here is 2Z02, the 11.37 Hooton to Helsby shuttle, passing Little Sutton station, which normally just sees Merseyrail Class 507 or 508 EMUs.

Freightliner Class 57 No. 57005 *Freightliner Excellence* waiting to depart the little-used Platform 4 at Hooton station with 1Z56, the 14.58 Crewe Circular Pathfinder railtour, on 1 June 2003. The train was top and tailed by an EWS Class 56, No. 56038, which brought the train into the station. No. 57005 is now residing at Carnforth as part of the WCRC non-operational fleet with No. 56038 at Leicester, awaiting its fate with Rail Operations Group.

Merseyrail Class 507 No. 507009 arrives at Birkenhead Central station on 15 July 2015 with 2Y23, the 16.12 Ellesmere Port to Liverpool Central and return train. The station was opened in 1886 as part of the route to Liverpool via the Mersey Railway Tunnel and was the headquarters of the Mersey Railway, which still stands today on Argyle Street. Next to the station is the disused building of the former three-road carriage shed, which closed in the 1990s.

On the former Hoylake Railway, Meols station opened in 1866 before becoming part of the Wirral Railway in 1883. When through services began to operate to Liverpool in 1938, the station, along with others along the line, was rebuilt into an art deco design, with Meols station being a good example of those on the line. Merseyrail Class 507 No. 507031 departs to Liverpool Central with 2W30, the 13.51 West Kirby and return train. 15 July 2015.

Arriva Trains Wales Class 150 No. 150253 waits to depart Bidston station after arrival a few minutes previously with 2F70, the 11.32 ex-Wrexham General. The station is the interchange between the Borders Line and Merseyrail, where trains go forward to West Kirby or Liverpool city centre. 15 July 2015.

On hire to Colas Rail from the Scottish 37 Group based at Bo'ness, Class 37 No. 37025 *Inverness TMD*, looking splendid in BR large logo livery, heads 3Q01, the 09.14 Shrewsbury to Crewe Carriage Sidings Network Rail Inspection train, through Upton station, Birkenhead. This station is operated by Arriva Wales West and is the first station after Bidston station on the Merseyrail system. This photograph was taken on a miserable 27 September 2016.

Fragonset Railways Class 47 No. 47701 *Waverley* approaches Harris Drive Bridge, Bootle, with 2Z01, the 10.55 Liverpool Lime Street to Aintree 'Inspection' special, on 8 April 2003. This location is on the now disused North Mersey Branch line that runs between Bootle Junction and Aintree station. The loco was part of the ScotRail push/pull fleet and was previously named *St Andrew*, but is now in two-tone green livery and is under the ownership of Nemesis Rail.

Top and tailed EWS Class 66s, led by No. 66100 with No. 66215 in the rear, is on 6L36, the 05.40 Crewe Basford Hall to Aintree 'Ballast' train, which is noted here dropping ballast on a renewed section of the North Mersey Branch line. Taken from Netherton Way Bridge, this location was the former site of Ford station, and to the right of the line was the former Aintree Container Depot. Nowadays this line has been very much mothballed, and in numerous locations nature is taking over the track bed. 22 August 2002.

Originally built by the East Lancashire Railway in 1849, Ormskirk station, although appearances deceive, is now a former shadow of itself, with now only one platform and a single line serving the station. Both Merseyrail and Northern trains terminate here but the line is separated by a buffer on each section. Seen here is Merseyrail Class 507 No. 507007, waiting to depart with 2G48, the 13.35 Ormskirk to Liverpool Central station. 3 June 2017.

In Network Rail yellow livery, Class 73 No. 73138 has just arrived at Platform 4, Southport station, with 2Q78, the 18.21 Wigan North Western and return recording train. At the other end of the train and leading back to Wigan is No. 73107. Southport station consists of six platforms, with three of them being dedicated to the Merseyrail electric service to Liverpool Central and Hunts Cross stations. 14 February 2012.

One of the nicest stations on the Northern line of the Merseyrail system is Birkdale, on the Southport to Liverpool Central line, which still retains the canopies, original station buildings and also the signal box, although this is hidden out of view in this image. Arriving at the station is Class 507 No. 507026 in Merseyrail silver livery with a late afternoon train to Hunts Cross. 8 September 2012.

It is rare, with the exception of engineering trains, that you see any type of loco-hauled train on the Merseyrail third rail system. 20 February 2008 was one of those occasions, when West Coast Railways Class 47s Nos 47826 and 47806 hauled 5Z02, the Carnforth to Hall Road and return ECS special. The combination is seen passing through Bootle Oriel Road station, which was being refurbished at the time, with Bootle Town Hall overlooking the station.

Just after a downpour, the sun comes out and a rainbow appears. Still in original two-tone grey livery with Mainline markings, Class 60 No. 60077, hauling a rake of ex-National Power JHA/JMA hoppers, passes Strand Road shunters cabin as it approaches Liverpool Bulk Terminal with 6F89, the ex-10.21 Fiddlers Ferry power station empty coal. Two hours later the loaded train would then be on its way back to the power station with another delivery of coal. 26 October 2001.

Taken from the EON's control tower at Liverpool Bulk Terminal, you get a birds-eye view of the surrounding area of Bootle and Liverpool along with the docks power station. By coincidence, in its unique Great Western green livery, Class 60 No. 60081 *Isambard Kingdom Brunel* arrives at the terminal with 6F79, the ex-15.05 Fiddlers Ferry power station empty JMA hoppers. This loco has now been dumped at DBS Toton depot, withdrawn and awaiting its fate. 29 August 2003.

History in the making when Pete Waterman's Class 46 No. 46035 (D172) *Ixion* was hired by Freightliner after a locomotive had derailed at the entrance of Crewe Basford Hall Yard. *Ixion* then proceeded to do two workings between Crewe and Seaforth Container Terminal as well as to Garston FLT. Just after arrival to the entrance of Seaforth CT, No. 46035 is seen on 29 May 1999 with 4P69, the ex-Garston FLT liner. This was the last occasion a Peak class locomotive visited Liverpool Docks.

In British Steel blue livery, EWS Class 60 No. 60006 *Scunthorpe Steelmaster* and one of two in this livery, the other being No. 60033 *Tees Steel Express*, is awaiting to depart Seaforth Container Terminal with 6Z53 to Cardiff Tidal. The train is very aptly loaded with imported steel coils for Allied Wire & Steel Ltd, Cardiff, who sadly went into receivership in 2002, with the locomotive being finally withdrawn in 2010 after only twenty years in service. 7 August 1998.

Although now owned by EWS, Class 56 No. 56007 is still in Transrail two-tone grey livery as it reverses 6P62, the ex-05.51 Walton Old Junction 'Cawoods' coal, into Seaforth Container Terminal on 2 July 2001. At that time coal was arriving in the distinctive yellow Cawoods open containers (on PFA flat wagons) from Onllwyn Washery, South Wales, and being exported to Ireland via Liverpool Docks.

Still in ex-works new EWS red livery, Class 60 No. 60097 reverses a late running 6F46, the ex-03.38 Arpley Sidings short 'Enterprise' service, across the road crossing into Seaforth Container Terminal. The Class 60 had been named *ABP Port of Grimsby & Immingham* two weeks previously at a naming ceremony at the port. Previously it had been in two-tone grey livery, with Transrail markings and was named *Pillar*. 28 March 2002.

Rebuilt and re-engined from Class 47 No. 47204 at Brush Traction only a few months previously, now Class 57 No. 57012 *Freightliner Envoy* approaches Strand Road crossing, Liverpool Docks, with 4K53, the 11.26 Seaforth Container Terminal to Crewe Basford Hall liner. The locomotive still survives today in the ownership and livery of Direct Rail Services. 17 June 2000.

Within a few months of this image being taken, this service to Stanton Grove, Atlantic Terminal, Liverpool Docks, ceased to operate and the traffic of paper rolls reverted back to road transport. EWS Class 66 No. 66185 is waiting to depart with 6F12, the 10.58 to Arpley Sidings, where it formed 6E33 to Immingham, where the paper rolls were imported from Europe. 9 October 2006.

Looking a bit weather-worn but still resplendent in Royal Scotsman livery, No. 37428 *Loch Long/Loch Awe* (one plate on either side) waits to depart Strand Road crossing, Liverpool Docks, with 6F56, the 12.06 Seaforth Container Terminal to Arpley Sidings empty Cawood boxes, on 20 January 2003. No. 37428 was withdrawn and scrapped at CF Booth, Rotherham, in 2013.

A scene that has changed beyond all recognition as the site of Liverpool Biomass Terminal: EWS Class 66 No. 66089 reverses its load of steel coils into Gladstone Steel Terminal on 1 May 2001. The train, formed of BYA carriers, originated from Lackenby, Teeside, and departed at 02.03 under reporting number 6M06.

Still in two-tone grey livery with 'Mainline' markings, Class 60 No. 60079 *Foinaven* shunts MBA wagons at EMR Alexander Dock Sidings, Liverpool Docks, prior to departing with the empty wagons as 6V72 to Washwood Heath. Happily the scrap traffic to the docks is still operated today, by DBS and recently GBRf, although, sadly, very rarely in daylight hours. 30 April 2004.

Now in EWS/Corus silver livery, Class 60 No. 60006 *Scunthorpe Ironmaster* is seen once again inside Liverpool Docks, this time forming 7F83, the 14.11 to Fiddlers Ferry power station coal. The train is reversing its mixed consist of forty-five HAA and HBA four-wheel wagons under the bunker of Liverpool Bulk Terminal, which is in the background. 28 March 2001.

Waiting to depart on 2 March 2001, EWS Class 56 No. 56059 idles in the sun with 6E82, the 12.42 Gladstone Steel Terminal via Healey Mills to Lackenby empty BYA wagons. In the background is EON's Liverpool Bulk Terminal and the line in the foreground is the connection to EMR Alexander Dock Sidings. No. 56059 eventually went to France as part of the Fertis fleet and was finally scrapped in 2011 at T. J. Thompson, Stockton.

Class 70 No. 70011, built by General Electric (USA), is busy reversing a rake of twenty-one HHA hoppers under the loading bunker of Liverpool Bulk Terminal. The train is then loaded with imported coal and forms 6Z59, the 14.55 to Ratcliffe power station. Behind the locomotive is the outline of the docks power station, which is powered by a Rolls-Royce engine similar to the RB211 engine that powers various passenger aircraft around the world. 8 August 2012.

An almost perfect reflection in a pond created by a heavy rain from the previous day. Transrail-liveried Class 60 No. 60035 *Florence Nightingale* draws the train of HBA hoppers slowly forward as it gets loaded with coal for Fiddlers Ferry power station. In the background is Liverpool Bulk Terminal, where the imported coal is being loaded, and this terminal has now been mothballed for the foreseeable future. 14 February 2001.

In reasonably clean two-tone Transrail livery, Class 60 No. 60085 is approaching Regent Road crossing prior to attacking the 1 mile, 1 in 60 climb to Bootle Junction with 7F80, the 07.43 Liverpool Bulk Terminal to Fiddlers Ferry power station. The 2,200-ton train consists of forty-five HAA four-wheel wagons loaded with imported coal. This part of Regent Road has now been incorporated as part of the dock estate and is no longer a through route to road traffic. 19 June 2000.

Having just departed from the docks, EWS Class 60 No. 60027, previously named *Joseph Banks*, puts the power on for the climb to Bootle Junction. The train, consisting of twenty-three loaded ex-National Power 'JMA' hoppers, is approaching Derby Road Bridge, Bootle, with 7F83, the 14.11 Liverpool Bulk Terminal to Fiddlers Ferry power station coal. You will note in the background that there is a stranded, crippled HAA wagon, which was eventually cut up on site. 8 August 2003.

As a contrast to the previous image, still the same location but almost fourteen years later, coal is no longer imported into Liverpool Docks, but rather biomass is instead, and a purpose-built terminal has been constructed. Here we have GBRf Class 66 No. 66716 *Locomotive and Carriage Institution Centenary 1911–2011* powering 6E10, the 11.23 Liverpool Biomass Terminal to Drax AES, with twenty-seven IIA 'Drax' hoppers loaded with biomass. In the background are the ship-to-shore red cranes, which form part of the new 'Liverpool 2' riverside dock quay. 8 May 2017.

In Mainline all-over blue livery, Class 60 No. 60011, with forty-five HBAs in tow, passes Bootle Junction and descends on the last mile to Liverpool Docks with 6P76, the 14.30 Fiddlers Ferry power station to Liverpool Bulk Terminal empties, on 18 May 1998. Under the bridge was the site of Bootle Balliol Road station, which closed in 1948, and on the horizon you are able to make out Liverpool's famous cathedrals. No. 60011 still operates today but in DB Schenker red livery.

Since 1990, as well as the Class 60s hauling the coal trains out of the docks, it was also a regular occurrence to see a pair of Class 56s on them too. In this view taken on 13 February 1998, Class 56s Nos 56082 and 56044 *Cardiff Canton QA* with 2,200 tonnes in tow finally make the top of the 1 in 60 incline to Bootle Junction and now wind their way onward to Edge Hill, and ultimately Fiddlers Ferry power station. In the foreground is the Merseyrail Northern line to and from Southport.

Passing Anfield Cemetery on the Bootle Branch line, EWS-liveried Class 66 No. 66149 disturbs the peace, hauling BYA and JSA wagons loaded with steel coils on 6F10, the 11.27 Arpley Sidings to Gladstone Steel Terminal. This location and view was only possible for a few months due to some cutting back and felling of trees by Network Rail. 8 March 2010.

This was certainly one of the last occasions where double-headed Class 56s were used on the Liverpool Bulk Terminal to Fiddlers Ferry power station coal trains. In EWS red livery, Nos 56117 and 56075 approach Edge Lane Bridge on the Bootle Branch Line. From here, they were routed via Edge Hill Wapping, Speke Junction, Ditton and Latchford Sidings before reaching the power station, where the author managed to record the train for the final time. 17 June 2000.

Approaching Edge Lane Bridge again, EWS Class 66 No. 66079 *James Nightall GC* on 6Z19, the 16.29 Seaforth Container Terminal to Arpley Sidings 'Aluminium Ingots', slows for Bootle Branch Junction to gain access to Tuebrook Sidings before proceeding on to Warrington. This train had only operated twice; therefore, the twenty VGA four-wheel vans were a rare sight on the branch. 18 May 2011.

Coming off the 300-metre Olive Mount chord at Edge Lane Junction, Class 60 No. 60074 *Teenage Spirit* begins to access the Bootle Branch line with 6F07, the 16.31 Walton Old Junction to Liverpool Bulk Terminal empty HTAs. The chord was unofficially closed in 1987 and was eventually lifted, but due to the increased levels of rail traffic to and from Liverpool Docks, a single bi-directional line was reinstated and became operational at the end of 2008. 7 August 2012.

On its third ownership and livery change, GBRf Class 66 No. 66745 *Modern Railways – The First 50 Years* takes the chord to Olive Mount Junction at Edge Lane Junction with 6G60, the 15.07 Liverpool Bulk Terminal to Ironbridge power station biomass. No. 66745 was previously operated by DRS as No. 66409, and then was transferred to Colas Rail as No. 66844 before coming under the ownership of GBRf in 2011. 23 April 2015.

On 3 May 2006, Class 66 No. 66151 crosses over at Waterloo Branch Junction to access Tuebrook Sidings prior to running around 6F10, the 14.25 Arpley Sidings to Gladstone Steel Terminal steel, before proceeding down to Liverpool Docks via the left-hand lines through Picko Tunnel No. 1. To the right of the lines, beyond the embankment, was the site of Edge Hill Steam Shed (8A) and in the background is Wavertree Technology Park station, which opened in 2000.

On a miserable autumn day, Class 66 No. 66011 reverses six loaded JXA wagons on a late-running 6F75 Arpley Sidings to EMR Alexander Dock scrap into the Victoria Tunnel entrance, Edge Hill, prior to taking it forward to Liverpool Docks. The lines that run down Victoria Tunnel, sometimes known as Waterloo Tunnel, went to Waterloo Dock and Liverpool Riverside station at the waterfront. The line was closed in November 1972, bar a short 500-metre stretch used as a head shunt at Edge Hill. 6 November 2007.

After running around its train at Edge Hill Wapping, in original Freightliner markings, Class 47 No. 47212 crosses onto the down line at Bootle Branch Junction with 4K74, the 11.19 Crewe Basford Hall to Seaforth Container Terminal liner. The train proceeds forward onto the Canada Dock Branch, more commonly known as the Bootle Branch, for the 5½-mile journey to Liverpool Docks. No. 47212 was built in 1965 as D1862 before being withdrawn in 2004. 18 July 1998.

Taken from the long-gone railway bridge that accessed the former Edge Hill Gridiron, RES-liveried Class 47 No. 47777 *Restored*, with InterCity livery Class 90 No. 90005 *City of London* dead in tow, heads the 12.15 Liverpool Lime Street to London Euston 'Sunday diversion'. The diversion was due to engineering work on the WCML, with the train now passing the site of Wavertree Technology Park station. 11 October 1998.

Taken from the bridge on Rathbone Road, having run around at Truebrook Sidings, Class 66 No. 66130 heads 6Z50, the 11.00 Seaforth Container Terminal to Gascoigne Wood empty Cawoods, through Wavertree Technology Park station. The station had only opened three weeks previously at a cost of £2 million, which includes ground level to platform level lifts and a booking office unusually located in the middle of the footbridge. 4 September 2000.

Virgin 'Thunderbird' Class 57 No. 57312 *Hood* drags Pendolino No. 390052 *Virgin Knight* on 1F16, the 12.06 London Euston to Liverpool Lime Street weekend WCML diversion, through Olive Mount Cutting on 9 July 2005. The sandstone cutting is 2 miles long, having been opened in 1830 with two tracks and widened in 1871 to take four tracks. By the time of this date, with the exception of the two running lines in this image, all other tracks, along with the junction to the Bootle Branch line, had all but disappeared.

Ten years later from the previous image, the junction to the Bootle Branch line had been reinstated albeit as a single bi-directional line and, more significantly, the electrification of the line had finally taken place. Seen here is former German-based Class 66 No. 66750 in GBRf plain livery approaching Rathbone Road Bridge with 4F61, the 13.00 Ironbridge power station to Tuebrook Sidings empty IIA hoppers. No. 66750 is now in full GBRf livery and named *Bristol Panel Signal Box*. 15 May 2015.

On 22 April 2011, former National Power-owned Class 59 No. 59202 *Vale of White Horse*, now in EWS ownership, takes the spur to the Bootle Branch line at Olive Mount Junction with a diverted 6F78, the 11.30 Fiddlers Ferry power station to Liverpool Bulk Terminal empty HTA hoppers. The EWS Class 59s were trialed on this diagram but were ultimately found unsuitable, and the trains reverted back to the trusty Class 60 locomotives.

Built in 2003, No. 66701 was initially the first of seven Class 66s for GB Railfreight and had been named *Railtrack National Logistics* and also *Whitemoor* too. Taken from Waldgrave Road footbridge, No. 66701 slows for the approach to Olive Mount Junction with 4M51, the 10.00 Drax AES to Liverpool Biomass Terminal empty biomass hoppers. With the electrification of the Liverpool and Manchester line photography from bridges has become a little more difficult, but fortunately this location seems to avoid the wires masking the train. 30 August 2016.

In attractive First TransPennine Express livery, a Siemens-built Class 185 DMU, No. 185151, approaches Bridge Road, Roby, with 1E71, the 12.12 Liverpool Lime Street to Newcastle Central train. This was taken during the reinstatement of the Up slow lines between Roby and Huyton to allow increased capacity, but before the electrification mast and wires were put up the following year by Network Rail. 17 July 2014.

In the early morning sunshine, GBRf No. 66730 *Whitemoor* on 4G01, the 05.51 Seaforth Container Terminal to Ironbridge power station containerised biomass, approaches Roby station on the new Up line as part of the reinstatement of the four tracks at this location. On the right is the track bed for the second Up (slow) line, which was laid later along with the realignment of both Roby and Huyton Junctions during the summer of 2017. 22 July 2014.

A scene that has changed beyond recognition is at Roby station, where the four platforms and lines that had been taken out in the late 1970s have now been reinstated, as well as full electrification too. This was the view before the work had commenced on 17 August 2011, where Freightliner Class 70 No. 70006, powering 6Z59, the 14.55 Liverpool Bulk Terminal to Ratcliffe power station loaded coal, is travelling on the former Up line. Happily the ex-LNWR station buildings, including the canopy, have been restored to their former glories.

Built in 1965 at Crewe Works as D1971, renumbered to No. 47270 and named *Cory Brothers 1842-1992* in 1996, is in the distance approaching Huyton Signal Box with a rare Freightliner working on this line as normally these trains are routed via Runcorn. In this instance, the train working is 4K58, the 15.30 Seaforth Container Terminal to Crewe Basford Hall liner, having just passed Roby station on 19 July 2004. Fortunately, No. 47270 still survives today in BR blue plain livery and occasionally operates on the main line for West Coast Railways.

As a contrast to the previous image and taken from a similar position, this is the current view with four lines and electrification all in place. Now the Down slow line, DRS Class 37 No. 37604, top and tail with No. 37419 *Carl Haviland 1954–2012*, approaches Roby station with Pathfinder's 'The Lancs Links' railtour, which visited various lines in the North West, starting and finishing at Crewe station. Three days after this image was taken the overhead wires were finally switched on and electric services began for the first time in the 185 years since the line was opened in 1830. 7 March 2015.

This was first occasion that a railtour had operated on this new section of line since it was opened: on 9 October 2017 Colas Rail Class 56 No. 56105, hauling Pathfinder's 'Fiddlers Five' Railtour with EWS Class 66 No. 66185 on the rear of the train, arrives at Platform Four, Huyton station. No. 56105 was heading the second leg of the tour, 1Z26 14.00 Ravenhead Sidings to Latchford Sidings, and was awaiting the passage of an EMT Class 158 on the Up fast line before following via the new crossover at Huyton Junction. 28 October 2017.

Approaching Huyton Signal Box on 4 March 2013, and in DB Schenker red livery, No. 60092 begins to increase the power for the attack on the one and half mile climb of Whiston incline with 6F74, the 12.11 Liverpool Bulk Terminal to Fiddlers Ferry power station coal. The signal box, unusually without a name board (missing at least since the 1970s), and closed as part of the resignalling and electrification of the line, was finally demolished during the weekend of 4 and 5 July 2014.

You would not think this was the same location but the common link with the previous image is the brick wall on the left-hand side, which is the only part of the surviving railway infrastructure in this view! Now on the Up fast line, DRS Class 57 No. 57310 *Pride of Cumbria* approaches Huyton station with the 'Northern Belle' tour of the North West with 1Z49, the 10.54 Crewe to Liverpool Lime Street, on 26 March 2017. On the rear of the train is No. 57312 *Solway Princess,* which is in Northern Belle livery.

All change and still awaiting 'Northern' decals, Class 319 electric unit No. 319366 departs from Huyton station on 8 May 2017 with 2F30, the 11.47 Liverpool Lime Street to Warrington Bank Quay train. Since this image was taken, and behind the train, the fourth (Up slow) line has been laid to allow a direct connection to the Prescot line at Huyton Junction, therefore giving the flexibility for trains to pass on the Up fast line to Rainhill and beyond.

Dominating the background skyline is the 331-foot tower of the Liverpool Anglican Cathedral as No. 60045 *The Permanent Way Institution* tackles the Whiston incline with its 2,100-ton load. The train, 6F81, the 09.14 Liverpool Bulk Terminal to Fiddlers Ferry power station coal, is approaching Pottery Lane Bridge, Whiston, which was the point of the railway connection to the long-gone Prescot Colliery. 26 March 2012.

Framed by the Grade II listed Dragon Lane Bridge (also known as Ropers Bridge), Whiston, EWS-liveried No. 60065 *Spirit of Jaguar* is working hard up the 1 in 99 incline with twenty-three loaded HTA hoppers on 6F74, the 12.11 Liverpool Bulk Terminal to Fiddlers Ferry power station coal. The sandstone bridge was designed and built in 1829 by George Stephenson. Along with the famous Skew Bridge, Rainhill, it is one of the earliest railway bridges in the world. 18 September 2012.

Still in its original two-tone grey paintwork, but with added Transrail logo and name, No. 60032 *William Booth* passes under Ropers Bridge and approaches Whiston station with 7F80, the 07.43 Liverpool Bulk Terminal to Fiddlers Ferry power station coal. This locomotive was built in 1990 by Brush Traction with Coal Sector markings and was stored in 2006 at DBC Toton, but since then has been sold to Wabtec for possible further use. 26 April 2003.

The driver of Royal locomotive No. 47799 *Prince Henry* is clearly making the Class 47 work hard while hauling the 10.10 Liverpool Lime Street to London Euston Sunday diversion, consisting of a DVT and nine Mk 3 coaches, and with a dead electric locomotive in tow. No. 47799, built in 1965, has had five identities in total including D1654 and Nos 47070, 47620 and 47835 *Windsor Castle*. It is now preserved at the Eden Valley Railway, Warcop. 8 October 2000.

On 12 November 2007, Class 37 No. 37411 (D6990) *Caerphilly Castle/Castell Caerffili*, looking splendid in British Railways green livery, works 6F14, the 09.27 Stanton Grove to Arpley Sidings empty VGAs, on the final approach to Whiston station. Built in 1965 at the English Electric Vulcan Foundry, this locomotive sadly met its fate in 2013 when it was withdrawn and scrapped.

On a cold, frosty morning, and approaching Whiston station, DRS Compass-liveried No. 47501 *Craftsman* heads 5Z45, the Crewe Basford Hall to Stoke-on-Trent (Sideway Loop) Driver Route Training move, consisting of six ex-Virgin Mk 2D/F coaches and with a dead Class 47, No. 47853, on the rear. No. 47501 was sold to Locomotive Diesels Ltd in 2014 and is now based at LNWR Crewe Diesel Depot, having been repainted in BR two-tone green livery and still being occasionally used. 16 January 2013.

With twenty minutes' notice, and running on a VSTP, an unusual rare move occurred on Sunday 20 March 2016, when an empty gypsum train passed Whiston station. This occurred due to operational issues at Fiddlers Ferry power station a couple of days previously, and the empty gypsum train, booked for Newbiggin, was diverted to Tuebrook Sidings for stabling pending onward movement. Seen here running under the wires are GBRf No. 66750 *Bristol Panel Signal Box* and No. 66718 *Sir Peter Hendy CBE,* hauling 4E10, the 12.24 Tuebrook Sidings to Doncaster Robert Roads Shed empty gypsum containers.

Although Class 221 Voyager units are not common visitors to Merseyside, very occasionally they are used to substitute Virgin Pendolinos on the Liverpool to London service, mainly for diversions. One such occasion was on 24 April 2011 when No. 221118 is seen passing the photographer's local station, Whiston, on 1H41, the 10.55 Liverpool Lime Street to Stockport 'Virgin' diversion, where the onboard passengers connected with an ex-Manchester Piccadilly Pendolino to London Euston station.

With twenty-three ex-powder blue National Power JMA loaded hoppers in tow, appropriately Mainline blue-liveried No. 60011 powers up Whiston incline to the summit at Rainhill as it approaches Cumber Lane Bridge, Whiston, on 30 March 2002 with 7F82, the 12.18 Liverpool Bulk Terminal to Fiddlers Ferry power station coal. No. 60011, now in DB Schenker red livery, was the last Class 60 to work a coal train on the circuit on 29 April 2015.

Taken from the same location as the previous image, Cumber Lane Bridge, work is proceeding to lower the track bed in preparation of the forthcoming electrification scheme as the bridge was one of the original structures on the line. In this view, No. 66623 *Bill Bolsover*, in Bardon Aggregates blue livery, is at the head of 6Y05, the 10.10 Crewe Basford Hall to Bootle Branch Junction ballast train. Freightliner No. 66546 is on the rear as the Orangemen discuss the next course of action on the Down line. 10 March 2012.

It is the beginning of spring with fresh snow on the ground, and DB Schenker red-liveried No. 60092 and its train of loaded coal now only has a half-mile climb before it reaches the summit at Rainhill, and then has the gentle journey to its destination of Fiddlers Ferry power station after leaving Liverpool Bulk Terminal at 09.14 under reporting code 6F81. Taken from Stoney Lane Bridge, this was the location of the engine house to provide cable assistance up the incline when the line originally opened. 25 March 2013.

Approaching Dee Road footbridge, and with only a few metres to go before 6F81, the 09.14 Liverpool Bulk Terminal to Fiddlers Ferry power station coal train, reaches the summit at Rainhill; No. 66075 would only then be able to slacken off. Occasionally, due to the unavailability of a Class 60, a Class 66 would be drafted onto the service, and although the train still consisted of twenty-three HTA hoppers, at least three of them would be empty for the journey to the power station as the usual load for a Class 66 would be too much on the climb out of the docks. 21 May 2012.

On the following day to the previous image, and at the next bridge on the line at Old Lane, Class 60 No. 60045 *The Permanent Way Institution*, with its matching rake of EWS hoppers, finally reaches Rainhill Level, the summit of the line from Liverpool, with the same 6F81 coal train to Fiddlers Ferry power station. 22 May 2012.

The first bridge to pass over a railway at an angle, the famous Skew Bridge at Rainhill station presents the backdrop for GBRf Class 66 No. 66716 *Cromer Lifeboat* on 6E09, the 07.53 Liverpool Biomass Terminal to Drax AES biomass, as it enters the station. The Grade II listed bridge was constructed at a 34 degree angle, was built by George Stephenson in 1829 and was made of red sandstone. 19 June 2017.

This image, taken before the wires were put into place, gives an overall view of one of the oldest railway stations in the world as TPEx Class 185 No. 185110 speeds through the Grade II listed Rainhill station with 1E66, the 09.12 Liverpool Lime Street to Newcastle Central service, on 12 June 2014. This was the site of the famous Rainhill Trials, held in 1829, where George Stephenson's *Rocket* won the competition to provide the locomotives for the newly constructed Liverpool & Manchester Railway, and there are display signs on the station to commemorate this historic event.

For a period in 2012, and as part of the electrification scheme, some bridges had to be raised for clearance purposes. In this instance, Network Rail took the opportunity to carry out some restoration work on the two footbridges at Rainhill station. This provided the chance of obtaining some rare shots without a footbridge in position. Taken from the main station footbridge, No. 60045 *The Permanent Way Institution* passes Rainhill Signal Box on 6F07, the 13.37 Fiddlers Ferry power station to Liverpool Bulk Terminal empty coal. 5 April 2012.

Passing Rainhill Signal Box and in Loadhaul livery, No. 60059 *Swinden Dalesman* powers 6F80, the 16.32 Fiddlers Ferry power station to Liverpool Bulk Terminal empty JMAs, on 17 September 2003. Looking at the previous image, you will note the signal box name board is still in place and the original 77 Steps footbridge in the background is still in position, which was the location of the 150th anniversary of the Liverpool & Manchester Railway celebrations in May 1980.

Withdrawn in 2010 after a period in France as part of the Fertis fleet, and sadly scrapped at EMR Kingsbury in 2012, Class 56 No. 56058 is seen in happier times approaching Rainhill 77 Steps footbridge with 6L32, the Tuebrook Sidings to Guide Bridge engineering train, on 1 November 2003.

With the WCML being closed for engineering work over the bank holiday weekend, and Liverpool FC playing at Wembley Stadium in the FA Cup final, LFC supporters had the opportunity of travelling by HST to watch the game. With one of two footexs that day, a rare opportunity of photographing an East Midlands Trains HST out of area and on my local line was too good to miss. With Rainhill station in the background, power cars No. 43061 and No. 43044 head 1Z42, the 09.26 Liverpool Lime St to London St Pancras 'Footex', on 5 May 2012.

Taken through the lattice frame of Rainhill 77 Steps footbridge, Northern Rail Class 156 DMU No. 156459 approaches with a Liverpool Lime St to Warrington Bank Quay service on a cold, frosty Friday morning. Over the course of the following weekend this footbridge was finally demolished, and along with it the many historic moments it had witnessed too. 2 March 2012.

Giving a good view of the Rainhill 77 Steps footbridge, and three other photographers taking advantage of its viewpoint, No. 60045 *The Permanent Way Institution* passes by on 6F81, the 09.00 Liverpool Bulk Terminal to Fiddlers Ferry power station loaded coal. At the rear of the train you can make out both Rainhill Signal Box and station. 14 January 2012.

On a nice summer's day, and now in DRS ownership, No. 37425, adorned with *Sir Robert McAlpine/Concrete Bob* name plates, hauls Inspection Saloon No. 975025 *Caroline* on a tour of Merseyside and Greater Manchester with 2Z02, the 09.32 Manchester Piccadilly via Liverpool Lime St and return special. Taken from the new footbridge at Rainhill Farm Fields, this new version has one less step compared with the previous lattice structure that spanned four lines. 16 August 2012.

Taken from the same position as the previous image, the wires are now in place, but using a short telephoto lens it is still possible to obtain an image at the Rainhill 76 Steps footbridge. GBRf No. 66721 *Harry Beck* in London Underground white livery approaches the footbridge with 6G64, the 08.00 Liverpool Bulk Terminal to Ironbridge power station loaded biomass. 11 March 2015.

Constructed in the mid-1980s, based on a Leyland National bus with ninety-six built in total, the Class 142 Pacer units were received with mixed results, but amazingly survived the test of time with some improvements, meaning that at least one of the units must be worthy of inclusion. Out of area and in Arriva Trains Wales livery, No. 142093 approaches 77 Steps footbridge in ideal snowy conditions with a Warrington Bank Quay to Liverpool Lime Street Northern Rail train. 6 January 2010.

During 2011, eighteen former London Midland Class 150 Sprinter units were transferred to Northern Rail including No. 150116 in attractive ex-Central Trains livery with yellow object deflector. Within a few weeks it was repainted into Northern Rail blue/purple livery with black-painted object deflector, which detracted from their appearance, and it is recorded as approaching 77 Steps footbridge on a morning Warrington Bank Quay to Liverpool Lime Street train. 12 November 2011.

Initially diverted to Arpley Sidings for operational reasons, an opportunity was presented to record this loaded train unusually during daylight hours. No. 60062 *Stainless Pioneer* approaches 76 Steps footbridge on a VSTP working, 6Z12, the 10.25 Arpley Sidings to Seaforth Container Terminal steel slabs for export to the USA. This train normally operates as 6M12 from Tinsley SS on a Thursday-only basis and has done so consistently for over twenty years, usually booked to arrive at the docks in the early hours of the following morning. 27 September 2013.

After turning at Earlestown triangle the empty coach stock and, in the rear, Great Western Castle No. 5043 *Earl of Mount Edgcumbe*, Class 47 D1755 (47773) in original two-tone BR green returns to Liverpool Lime Street station as it approaches 77 Steps footbridge on 1 October 2011. The train had originally arrived at Lime Street station led by No. 5043 from Birmingham on the 'Ticket to Ride' railtour and necessitated going to Earlestown in order for the steam locomotive to be facing the right direction for the return to Birmingham.

On the Rainhill Level, the actual site of the Rainhill Locomotive Trials in 1829, General Electric-powered No. 70016 in Freightliner Powerhaul livery passes by with 4Z59, the 11.13 Crewe Basford Hall to Liverpool Bulk Terminal empty HHA hoppers, on 2 March 2012. This train, upon arrival at Liverpool Docks, is then loaded with coal to form 6Z59 to Ratcliffe power station, returning via the same route and passing Rainhill at 15.45.

In EWS livery with a matching rake of empty HTAs, No. 59205 *L. Keith McNair* ambles along the Rainhill Level with 6F09, the 17.15 Fiddlers Ferry power station to Liverpool Bulk Terminal empty coal. No. 59205 is one of six built by General Motors, La Grange, Illinois, USA, in 1995 for National Power to haul their JMA hoppers supplying coal to their generating power stations. The locomotives and hoppers were eventually taken over by EWS in 1998. 3 August 2011

In the golden hour on a late autumn afternoon, 16 November 2003, Virgin-liveried Class 57 Thunderbird No. 57303 *Alan Tracy* powers 1A60, the 15.15 Liverpool Lime Street to London Euston Sunday diversion, past the 77 Steps footbridge on the Rainhill Level. On the rear of the train is Class 90 No. 90001 *BBC Midlands Today*, which will take over the when it reaches Stockport station and power the train on to London Euston.

Taken adjacent to the previous picture and in early springtime, the sun sets on the north side of the line. The first Class 60 to appear in DB Schenker red livery, No. 60011 passes the footbridge on 6F84, the 16.56 Liverpool Bulk Terminal to Fiddlers Ferry power station loaded HTAs, on 25 March 2011. DB Schenker had decided to overhaul up to twenty Class 60s at that time with an upgrade but, contrary to belief, No. 60011 only received an electrical upgrade, with No. 60007 having the honour of being the first to be completely overhauled, then being known as a Super Tug.

On the Rainhill Level, No. 170399, operated by Central Trains in Birmingham City of Culture livery, is on the last few miles of the 09.22 Nottingham to Liverpool Lime Street diversion on 3 October 2003. Built in Derby between 1998 and 2005 by Bombardier Transportation, 122 Class 170 Turbostar sets were constructed in two- or three-car configuration. This particular Turbostar was promoting the city of Birmingham's bid to become European City of Culture in 2008, but sadly for them it was awarded to the city of Liverpool, with great benefit to the city.

As the first two trial attempts to run a biomass train to Drax AES from Liverpool Bulk Terminal were cancelled, the third occasion operated on 1 February 2014. Consisting of twenty-seven Drax and plain-liveried biomass hoppers, and double-headed by No. 66735 and No. 66741 *Swanage Railway*, they power across the level at 08.55 with sunrise being less than an hour before. As the train had been loaded the day before at Liverpool Bulk Terminal, it departed from Tuebrook Sidings at 08.30 under reporting code 6H64.

This book would not be complete without the author's favourite Class 60 No. 60057 *Adam Smith* appearing and, in this instance, approaching the St Helens Linkway (A570) road bridge on 7F81, the 10.11 Liverpool Bulk Terminal to Fiddlers Ferry power station loaded coal. This locomotive remained in two-tone grey livery with coal sector markings for all but one year of its twenty-year active life. The area behind the train is now a large housing estate. 16 August 2003.

Passing the original site of Lea Green station, which closed in September 1958, Class 67 No. 67024 heads towards Rainhill on 6F10, the 14.25 Arpley Sidings to Gladstone Steel Terminal steel coils in BYA and JSA wagons, on 4 May 2006. Although Class 67s visited Merseyside regularly, it was rare to see them on any type of freight train but this service did produce the occasional one. No. 67024 has now been repainted into VSOE Pullman livery as one of two dedicated locomotives for the British Pullman which operates out of London.

In experimental Northern Rail livery, Class 156 Super Sprinter No. 156451 approaches the bridge on Lea Green Road with a morning Liverpool Lime Street to Manchester Airport train. This location was the site of the original Lea Green station, which had staggered platforms with the Down Liverpool-bound platform adjacent to the DMU and the Up platform on the other side of the bridge. 4 April 2007.

Looking east off Lea Green Road Bridge, and with the new Lea Green station in the distance, unnamed No. 60091 hauls its train of empty HTAs towards the Rainhill Level with 6F07, the 13.45 Fiddlers Ferry power station to Liverpool Bulk Terminal, on the late spring afternoon of 28 May 2012. No. 60091 was built in 1992 and named *An Teallach* until it was repainted into DB Schenker livery, then being named *Barry Needham* in 2014.

Former Dutch grey Class 66 No. 66749, now in GBRf markings, approaches Lea Green station on 6G64, the 08.00 Liverpool Bulk Terminal to Ironbridge power station biomass, on 24 April 2015. No. 66749 was purchased along with two other unused Class 66s from Crossrail Benelux (who originally ordered them in late 2012) by GBRf, and after some modifications they were put into traffic still in their grey livery, numbered 66747–749. They were eventually repainted into the attractive GBRf blue and yellow livery.

Having reached the summit of the line at Rainhill, No. 60060 *James Watt*, in coal sector markings, now takes it easy on the descent to St Helens Junction as it passes Lea Green station, which had opened less than a year earlier. It is seen here on 7F82, the 10.11 Liverpool Bulk Terminal to Fiddlers Ferry power station loaded coal, comprising a mixture of HAA and HBA four-wheel wagons. 12 May 2001.

On a lovely summer's evening, No. 66216 climbs the Sutton incline from St Helens Junction as it approaches Marshall's Cross road bridge, Lea Green. The train, consisting of five JXA open wagons, is on 6F74, the 18.23 Arpley Sidings to EMR Alexander Dock loaded scrap, which can be clearly seen in this view. No. 66216 is now part of the Euro Cargo Rail fleet, based in Alizay, France. 23 June 2005.

Still looking to be in ex-works condition, and having been renamed two months earlier to *Spirit of Jaguar*, No. 60065, on 7F80, the 08.18 Liverpool Bulk Terminal to Fiddlers Ferry power station coal, passes Sutton Leach on 10 May 2003. Behind the photographer was the first railway-over-railway bridge in the world, built when the St Helens & Runcorn Gap Railway was constructed in 1833, crossing over the Liverpool & Manchester Railway at this particular point. Sadly there is almost no trace of this historical intersection.

Previously in two-tone grey Construction Sector livery and named *Glastonbury Tor*, No. 60039 passes St Helens Junction station on 6F09, the 17.07 Fiddlers Ferry power station to Liverpool Bulk Terminal empty coal. Since 2015, when the locomotive was overhauled and repainted into DB Schenker livery, it has been named *Dove Holes*. Although the station still has 'Junction' as part of the name, it has been a long time since it was a junction connecting with the ex-St Helens & Runcorn Gap Railway. 7 August 2013.

Probably the most colourful locomotive on the national network, and in what is best described as rainbow livery, GBRf No. 66720 races through St Helens Junction station with 6G60, the 08.00 Liverpool Bulk Terminal to Ironbridge power station biomass, on 10 June 2014. The livery was designed by schoolchildren as part of a competition organised by GBRf, with each side of the locomotive bearing a different colourful design.

In the early days of the luxury dining train operator Northern Belle, they hired in Deltic No. 55019 *Royal Highland Fusilier* to haul their train. On 10 June 2000, it is seen here passing St Helens Junction station with the 08.00 Liverpool Lime Street to Grantham and return railtour.

Another view of the author's favourite Class 60: No. 60057 *Adam Smith* is seen approaching St Helens Junction station from the east on 6F80, the 18.32 Walton Old Junction to Liverpool Bulk Terminal empty JMAs. It is hard to imagine that over thirty years ago Bold power station and the Colliery existed in the background when the only sign of any existence of the latter is the earth mound in the background, which is the site of one of the spoil tips. Bold Colliery sadly closed in 1985. 3 July 2003.

Passing the site of Bold Colliery on the left, No. 60045 *The Permanent Way Institution* approaches Broad Lane Bridge, Collins Green, with 6F81, the 09.14 Liverpool Bulk Terminal to Fiddlers Ferry power station loaded HTAs, on 29 March 2013.

The nine arches of the Sankey Viaduct, being the earliest major railway viaduct in the world, built by George Stephenson between 1828 and 1830, carry the Liverpool & Manchester Railway over Sankey Brook and the former canal. Passing over the Grade I listed structure is a Northern Electric-liveried Class 319 EMU with 1H48, the 12.16 Liverpool Lime Street to Manchester Airport. 25 October 2010.

Having been built nearby at the former Vulcan Foundry in 1961, Deltic D9000 (No. 55022) *Royal Scots Grey* passes Earlestown station with the Deltic Preservation Society's 'The TransPennine Deltic' railtour from London Kings Cross to Liverpool Lime Street station on 18 October 1997. The station building on the island platform is the oldest station building in the world still in passenger use, having opened in 1835.

Nicely matching the livery of Drax biomass hoppers, Aggregates Industries-liveried GBRf Class 66 No. 66711 *Sence* passes through Earlestown station on a nice summer's evening with 4M09, the 16.28 Drax AES to Liverpool Biomass Terminal empties. 12 July 2017.

A lightly loaded Network Rail train consisting of Track Recording Coach DB999508, headed by DRS Class 37 No. 37261 and with NR-owned Class 31 No. 31105 at the rear, passes Earlestown station on 2Q88, the Wigan Spring Branch to Derby Railway Technical Centre train. The train was slowing down to enter the Earlestown West bi-directional loop before heading to Warrington Bank Quay station, then returning and travelling onward to Liverpool Lime Street on 27 June 2012.

In Fastline livery, but now in DRS ownership, Class 66s Nos 66304 and 66301 approach Newton-le-Willows station on 0Z16, the Gresty Bridge to York 'Route Training', on 4 March 2011. The locomotives are crossing Newton Viaduct, built by George Stephenson in 1828, two years before the line opened. For a brief period in 2008 and 2009 Fastline operated some coal trains between Liverpool Bulk Terminal and Ratcliffe power station, but parent company Jarvis went into administration in 2010. (Image courtesy of Mark Youdan)

On an Arriva Trains Wales service, DB Schenker red-liveried Class 67 No. 67015 arrives at Newton-le-Willows station with 1D31, the 16.50 Manchester Piccadilly to Llandudno train, on 24 August 2016. The Grade II listed, two-storey station building was opened in 1845 by the London & North Western Railway and still retains its canopy, and at the time of writing the station is being partially redeveloped.

With Vulcan Village in the background, GBRf No. 66730 *Whitemoor* approaches Winwick Junction on the Up Earlestown line with 6G64, the 08.00 Liverpool Bulk Terminal to Ironbridge power station biomass. Three months later these trains ceased to operate as Ironbridge power station finally became life expired and was closed. 8 August 2015.

At the time this image was taken it was unusual to see electric-hauled trains on this section of line from Earlestown South Junction, and much to my surprise this south-bound Cross Country appeared headed by Class 86 No. 86258 *Talyllyn – The First Preserved Railway* with No. 86225 *Hardwicke* dead in tow, on the approach to Winwick Junction. Apparently the section of the WCML between Golborne Junction and Winwick Junction had been closed, with all trains being diverted via Newton-le-Willows and the Earlestown East curve. 18 October 1998.

Approaching Winwick Junction in the low evening sunshine, preserved Class 40 No. 40145 (D345), owned by the Class 40 Preservation Society, passes its birth place at Vulcan Foundry with 1Z42, Pathfinder's 16.40 York (ex-Newcastle-upon-Tyne) to Birmingham 'The Whistling Tynesider' railtour, on 5 April 2003. The locomotive was built in 1961 and normally resides at the East Lancashire Railway between railtours.

With Fiddlers Ferry power station dominating the skyline, No. 92036 *Bertolt Brecht,* built by Brush Traction in 1995 and still in two-tone original grey livery with EWS markings, makes light work of 4S43, the 07.30 Daventry to Mossend intermodal train, as it attacks the climb to Golborne Junction at Redbank. Nowadays this train is operated by Direct Rail Services and is mostly now in the hands of the new Class 88 electric locomotives. 26 May 2012.

Powered by two DB Cargo Class 90s, No. 90036 *Driver Jack Mills* and No. 90026, the latter still in EWS livery, 4M25, the 06.06 Mossend to Daventry intermodal train, descends to Winwick Junction at Redbank, Newton-le-Willows, on the morning of 23 April 2015.

Appearing from under the farmer's occupation bridge at Redbank, Newton-le-Willows, and in miserable autumn light on 7 October 2017, two British Rail Class 50s, No. 50007 (D507) *Hercules* and No. 50049 *Defiance,* make a wonderful sight and sound as they power 1Z50, the 06.10 London Euston to Glasgow Central 'Caledonian' Pathfinder railtour, complete with appropriate headboard. Both Class 50s were passing the site of Vulcan Foundry, where they were built in 1968, and they used to be a common occurence up and down the WCML in the early 1970s.

In early springtime evening light, No. 56087 in Colas livery brings its load of timber in IWA bogie wagons pass Redbank, Newton-le-Willows, with 6J37, the 12.40 Carlisle Yard to Chirk (North Wales), on 12 March 2014. Since Colas Rail took over this service from EWS, they have used double-headed Class 56s, a single Class 60 and 66, and Class 70s in hauling this particular train.

Class 08 No. 08202, in the yellow livery of Potter Logistics Ltd, brings 6E30, the 11.00 Knowsley to Immingham empty VGAs, down the Headbolt Lane shunt line at Kirkby prior to being taken forward by an EWS locomotive to its destination on 21 August 2002. No. 08202 is currently at the Avon Valley Railway and was built in 1956 at Derby Works as D3272.

Following on from the previous image, but this time taken from Dale Lane Bridge, Kirkby, on the former Lancashire & Yorkshire Liverpool to Wigan Wallgate line, No. 56099, formerly named *Fiddlers Ferry Power Station* *and* still in two-tone grey Transrail livery, accelerates away with the train on the single-line section to Rainford Junction on 21 August 2002.

Taken at Rainford station after handing in the single line token at Rainford Junction signal box, Class 56 No. 56018 in EWS livery departs with 6E30, the 11.00 Knowsley (Potters) to Immingham empty VGAs, on to the double-line section to Wigan Wallgate on 22 August 2001. Although managed by Arriva Northern in 2017, Rainford station is included as part of the Merseytravel public transport area, hence its inclusion in this book.

Sixteen years after the previous image, and taken from Rainford station footbridge, the driver of EWS-liveried No. 66014 hands the single line token to the Rainford Junction signalman before departing with 6E16, the 10.59 Knowsley Freight Terminal to Wilton EFW Terminal waste disposal train. Looking closer at the signal box, it has been subject to some work by Network Rail with PVC cladding, new windows and the reappearance of the signal box name board. 12 July 2017.

On a pleasant summer's evening, Class 66 No. 66031 powers across Carr Mill Viaduct, St Helens, with a rake of DB-liveried MMA wagons on 6 June 2016. This train is 6Z82, the 17.49 Ravenhead Sidings to Arpley Sidings empties, with the inbound train normally delivering sand for Pilkington Glass at St Helens once a week. This section of line was originally opened by the Lancashire Union Railway in 1869 before being taken over by the London & North Western Railway.

Passing St Helens Signal Box, Class 319 EMU No. 319366, in Northern Electric livery, approaches St Helens Central station with 2F63, the 18.03 Wigan North Western to Liverpool Lime Street train. The area around the signal box was full of extensive sidings, but as time has gone by they have either been redeveloped or reclaimed by nature, as seen in the background of this image. 9 May 2016.

A busy scene at St Helens Central station as two Northern Electric Class 319 EMUs cross each other on 9 May 2016. Having arrived a minute earlier, No. 319380 awaits to depart with 1N84, the 11.03 Liverpool South Parkway to Preston, as No. 319382 approaches on 2F65, the 11.31 Wigan North Western to Liverpool Lime Street train. The station was renamed from St Helens Shaw Street in 1987 with the original GCR Central station being closed in 1952, and during 2007 it was subject to a complete rebuild, costing £6 million.

Operating two hours late, and in unmarked EWS livery, No. 66109, with a train of ten JXA bogie wagons loaded with sand, and operating 6Z81, the 08.38 Arpley Sidings to Ravenhead Sidings (Pilkington's Glass) train, crosses St Helens station junction at midday on 9 May 2016. Taken from Parr Street Bridge, the line beneath is the former St Helens Railway, which was cut back as far as Sutton Oak. The last trains travelled the line in 2002, and since then this section has been out of use.

Approaching St Helens station junction, and crossing the St Helens Canal, Class 66 No. 66089 makes a nice reflection while on 6F88, the Sutton Oak (Hays Chemical) to Arpley Sidings tanks, on 19 January 2001. This section of the canal is known as The Hotties due to the warm water pumped out by the nearby Pilkington Glass Factory and is a popular fishing spot for local anglers.

On the now mothballed section of the former St Helens & Runcorn Gap Railway at Peasley Cross run round loop, No. 37040 heads Pathfinder's 'The Ribble Nibble' railtour, which originated from Swindon and carried out a tour of lines in the North West. At the rear of the train was No. 37293, which took the train as far as the Network Rail boundary at Hays Chemicals, Sutton Oak, 250 metres beyond the background bridge. 1 August 1998.

Coming off the junction, EW&S-liveried No. 37704, hauling two TDA Tiphook bogie tanks, enters St Helens Central station as it heads to Arpley Sidings with 6F88, the ex-11.02 to Sutton Oak, on 16 August 2002. The following month this service ceased due to the Hays Chemicals factory closing, and with that the line to Sutton Oak saw its last train. Since then the line has become overgrown with vegetation, but it is still part of Merseytravel's wish list to reopen it one day to St Helens Junction.

Having left the 80-yard-long Scholes Tunnel, West Coast Railways Class 47 No. 47760 climbs to the summit on the St Helens Central to Huyton Junction line while heading 1Z83, the 16.11 Carlisle to Liverpool Lime Street 'Railway Touring Company' railtour, as it approaches Eccleston Park station on 30 July 2012.

In Hunslet Barclay livery, Class 20 No. 20902 *Lorna* heads the Seaforth CT to Wigan Springs Branch weedkiller train with Class 20 No. 20903 *Alison* at the rear after passing Prescot station and signal box on 26 July 1996. Behind the train is the former BICC works and railway sidings, which in the next image have since disappeared! Since the late 1980s and early 1990s, with the exception of the WCML that goes through Newton-le-Willows, Class 20 locomotives have been rare visitors to the region; the last known to appear were No. 20305 and No. 20308 in mid-2015 on driver route training from Liverpool Docks.

With nine coaches in tow, LMS-built Black 5 No. 45305 approaches Warrington Road Bridge, Prescot, with 1Z42, the 07.25 Liverpool Lime Street to Carlisle 'Cumbrian Mountain Express' railtour. In the background you are able to make out Prescot Signal Box and to the right of the train was the site of the extensive BICC works, which is now occupied by apartments. No. 45305 is displaying the 8A shed plate as she was once allocated to Edge Hill MPD in BR steam days. 23 July 2011.

What was once one of the classic shots on this line: West Coast Railways Class 47 No. 47826 passes Prescot Signal Box with 5Z48, the Preston to Liverpool Lime Street ECS, on 25 June 2009. This stock had travelled to Preston for stabling as part of the NENTA 'Manchester & Liverpool Explorer' railtour from Norwich to Liverpool and back. Since this image was taken the signal box and signalling have now gone due to the electrification upgrade of the line.

It was rare to see any freight train on this section of line since the demise of the trains to and from BICC in the late 1980s as it is primary a commuter line. On Sunday 4 August 2013, due to engineering works on the L&M line, GBRf No. 66724 *Drax Power Station* is approaching Prescot station on a diverted 4F66, the 17.33 Ironbridge power station to Tuebrook Sidings empty biomass. The site of the signal box is behind the locomotive.

This book cannot be completed without the latest locomotive class to hit the shores of the UK; namely, the Direct Rail Services Electro/Diesel Class 88, built by Stadler Rail, with the capacity to draw its power from an overhead line or a built-in diesel engine. No. 88002 *Prometheus,* which was the first of the class to arrive, in January 2017, passes Prescot station on 0Z89, the 11.04 Crewe to Carlisle Kingmoor route/driver training light engine move, on 28 March 2017.

The final image in this book brings up to date as far as motive power is concerned, with DRS No. 88002 *Prometheus* being the first Class 88 to haul a passenger-carrying train. No. 88002 is seen here passing Redbank, Newton-le-Willows (WCML), on a sunny spring evening hauling UK Railtours' 'The Class 88 VIP Railtour', 1Z89 16:40 Carlisle to London Euston, comprising the 'Northern Belle' coaching stock. On the rear was another DRS locomotive, Class 68 No. 68022 *Resolution,* which provided ECS assistance at Carlisle and London. 9 May 2017.